Social Media Marketing

Leverage the Power of the Internet to Grow Your Business

By K. Connors

Table of Contents

K. Connors

Platforms for Social Media Marketing

Some of the best social media platforms for business, like Facebook and Instagram, have become essential tools in the modern marketer's toolbox. More and more consumers are using these channels to find new companies and engage with their favorite brands. However, most companies can't be everywhere at once, especially small businesses with tight marketing budgets. That's why it is vital for businesses to be strategic about which social media platforms they work to build a presence on.

The key to successful social media marketing in the coming year will be choosing the best social media platform for your business. This is based on a number of factors, including the type of business you have, what audience you are trying to reach, your specific goals, and much more.

Below, we've put together a quick and simple guide to choosing the best social media for business.

Facebook

This is the biggest social media network on the Internet, both in terms of total number of users and name recognition. Founded on February 4, 2004, Facebook has, within 12 years managed to accumulate more than 1.59 billion monthly active users and this automatically makes it one of the best mediums for connecting people from all over the world with your business. It is estimated that more than 1 million small and medium-sized businesses use the platform to advertise their business.

Twitter

You might be thinking that limiting your posts to 140 characters is no way to advertise your business, but you will be shocked to know that this social media platform has more than 320 million active monthly users who make use of the 140 character limit to pass on information. Businesses can use Twitter to interact with prospective clients, answer questions, release latest news and at the same time use the targeted ads with specific audiences. Twitter was founded on March 21, 2006, and has its headquarters in San Francisco, California.

LinkedIn

Founded on December 14, 2002, and launched On May 5, 2003, LinkedIn is hands-down the most popular social media site for professional networking. The website is available in 24 languages and has over 400 million registered users. LinkedIn is great for people looking to connect with people in similar industries, networking with local professionals and displaying business related information and statistics.

Google+

While it's no Twitter, Facebook or LinkedIn, Google+ has its place among the popular social media sites. Its SEO value alone makes it a must-use tool for any small business. Launched on   December 15, 2011, Google+ has joined the big leagues registering 418 active million users as of December 2015.

YouTube

YouTube - the largest and most popular video-based social media website - was founded on February 14, 2005, by three former PayPal employees. It was later bought by Google in November 2006 for $1.65 billion. YouTube has over 1 billion website visitors per month and is the second most popular search engine behind Google.

Pinterest

Launched in March 2010, Pinterest is a relative newcomer in the social media arena. This platform consists of digital bulletin boards where businesses can pin their content. Pinterest announced September 2015 that it had acquired 100 million users. Small businesses whose target audience is mostly made up of women should definitely invest in Pinterest as more than half of its visitors are women.

Instagram

Like Pinterest, Instagram is a visual social media platform. The site, launched on October 6, 2010, has more than 400 million active users and is owned by Facebook. Many of its users use it to post information about travel, fashion, food, art and similar subjects. The platform is also distinguished by its unique filters together with video and photo editing features. Almost 95 percent of Instagram users also use Facebook.

Tumblr

Tumblr is one of the most difficult to use social networking platforms, but it's also one of the most interesting sites. The platform allows several different post formats, including quote posts, chat posts, video and photo posts as well as audio posts, so you are never limited in the type of content that you can share. Like Twitter, reblogging, which is more like retweeting, is quick and easy.

The social networking website was founded by David Karp in February 2007 and currently hosts more than 200 million blogs.

Why Choose Social Media

Fifteen years ago when a business wanted to market their products or service to an audience, the most viable options were print marketing or television and radio advertising. Websites were slowly making their way into the mainstream for business, and people were hesitantly boarding the internet train one-by-one. Fast forward to 2019 and the ways in which businesses can market to their customers have changed tremendously.

Websites for businesses are now more than mainstream, they've become a necessity. Millions of customers use search engines to find everything they need to know about a business before even making a purchase. Videos are the new shiny attention-getters, and anyone who is anyone has a Twitter or Facebook account to keep up with their friends, acquaintances, and loved ones.

With all of these rapidly made advancements in technology, a door has been opened not only for internet users and individuals to entertain and educate themselves, but also for businesses to enter the market of online advertising and keep their business in the forefront of their customers' minds. Let's look at the many ways in which social media can help you connect, engage, and grow your business.

1. Target Your Customer Audience

Social media gives you the opportunity to target your target audience directly via several different networking channels. The social media networks that you choose to use will be determined by your customer audience.

For example, if your primary target market is teens and young adults ages 15-30, Instagram would be a great social media platform to communicate your value as a business. It is highly visual, includes video capabilities, and has produced great return on investment figures from customer contests.

According to Actionable Marketing Guide, 71% of the world's internet users are on Facebook, which amounts to an astoundingly large potential audience for your profile. Businesses can expect great rewards from posting frequently and including a variety of content on their page, including videos, images, and links.

Twitter is largely used for mass marketing tactics that include articles, images, links, and the ever-popular hashtag. Teens and young adults are heavily consuming the market of Twitter, however, some older adults can also be found on this platform. Having a 140 character limit per tweet keeps a business's posts short, sweet, and to the point for their consumer.

If you're interested in targeting women ages 18-49, Pinterest is the social media network for you, as 41% of women on the internet frequent this site. It's popular for do-it-yourself crafts and projects, however, businesses are seeing great results from posting their products, services, ideas, and other items on Pinterest to pull that market into their business. In fact, Pinterest is the second largest referrer of social media traffic for businesses.

LinkedIn is a highly professional and business-oriented social media. I like to say it's Facebook with a suit on. Business-to-business companies should certainly be on this platform to build brand awareness, gain sales leads, and connect with potential partners and opportunities. Having a company page and posting unique, valuable content to that page regularly is what separates your business from the competition.

Finally, Google+ is a social network that gets an unpopular reputation of only being used by Google employees. This couldn't be more false. Google+ is a network that if used in conjunction with a Google My Business page can result in instant gratification for your customers and increase search engine optimization for your website and your business.

2. Turn "Likes/Followers" into Customers

The biggest challenge business owners face once acquiring social media platforms is using them! The key to increasing your customers online is interacting with them via posts that can include images, links, videos, articles, and text. The more frequent you post, the better. Customers want to have a reason to interact with a business, and many companies use videos, customer testimonials, contests, and discounts to pull customers from their social media profiles to their websites and/or storefronts.

3. Broadcast Brand Awareness

One of the most common reasons a business might be on social media is to establish and spread awareness for their brand. In today's ages of technology, having a Facebook or a Twitter account for your business shows that you're a "real" business that is advancing just as quickly as the technology with which you are keeping up. It is the equivalency of having a logo or a business card for your business. Customers view your profiles and then judge your business and your brand based on the type of content, frequency with which you post, and the amount of opportunities for value that you offer your customers on your profiles, whether this be articles, discounts, contests, videos, etc.

The important thing to remember about brand awareness is that your profile needs to look as professional and aesthetically pleasing as it can be; this includes having your logo as a profile picture, choosing an attention-getting cover photo, and your business information being complete and accurate in your profile.

There are so many ways social media can help improve the marketing of your business. This chapter is just the tip of the iceberg of social media marketing methods. Continue reading and you'll learn how you can take your business to the next level with social media.

Finding A Target Market

Ask yourself this: who is the audience at the receiving end of your marketing efforts?

As much as your product or service may appeal to a large group of people, it doesn't make sense to market to everyone. You obviously want as many people to know about your business as possible, but the more potential customers you want to reach, the more time, effort, and money it is going to cost to do so.

Depending on your brand or the objectives of the campaign, specific audiences may hold a higher value to you. Targeting high-value groups for your business and customizing messaging to reach particular audiences leads to a higher ROI (return on investment). Rather than digging through a haystack in hopes of finding a needle, you can adjust your campaign messaging to be like a magnet that brings the needle, your target audience, to you.

Even today, marketing digitally without knowing how to find your target audience can waste time and energy, which can affect your bottom line significantly. A target audience is an audience that, when you reach them, are more likely to convert to sales because their purchasing interests coincide with what you are selling.

By selecting different target audiences, and focusing on the portion of the people who would be most interested in your products or services, you are allowing yourself to communicate and engage with that segment more personally.

Follow this step-by-step process to identify your target audience, based on where you are now, and where you want to be in future campaigns.

1. Consult Your Business Plan

When you are identifying your target audience, it is important also to determine the features of your product or service. What needs does your product or service fulfill for a potential customer? How does your product or service differ from other products or services in your industry? Is your product more affordable? Is it more effective? You must take many of these things into account before figuring out who will be on the receiving end of your marketing efforts. Think about who might be interested and who may benefit from having access to what you offer. These are the people that will make up your target audience.

Keep in mind when thinking about how to market to your target audience that today's consumers don't like to be "sold to." They are much savvier than consumers of the past. Between television advertising, print ads and all the various forms of advertising on the internet, they've seen it all. They want to be informed and entertained. They want to be in control of their buying experience. By learning how to identify your target audience and marketing to that group, you are giving them that control.

If you are already in business, defining your target audience can be as easy as looking at your best customers. Who are they, and what traits do they have in common? Do you have more success selling to a particular demographic? Who do you want to get in front of, and what do you already know about this group of people?

2. Research

Regardless of marketing, you must know your competitors well to make an impact in your current market. But to find your target audience, and what they want, you will also need to better understand the competition. Pull together relevant information about your industry, the market, your competition, and most importantly, the broad potential customer you have identified. How have your competitors marketed their products/services, and to whom?

Another source to finding your target audience is your existing or best customers. If you want to find more of these people (and grow your customer base), find out what makes them tick. What interests them? How did they find out about your product/service? What did they like or dislike about it? The more information you have, the easier it is to identify and reach your target audience.

If you already have access to a data management platform, you should consult the audience analytics you have available to learn even more. For example, Lotame's Audience Profile Report can give additional insights into your target audience's behaviors, interests, actions, and demographics across screens. All of this information should be combined as you build your target audience for a holistic view and understanding of the consumer. You are essentially creating a comprehensive or nearly complete profile of the kind of customer you are targeting.

3. Find Your Target Audience

As you might expect, it helps to identify and understand the broader market you are after, before narrowing it down to specifics. The process is as follows:

- Look at existing marketing strategies

- Identify existing customer groups or segments
- Review your competition and other businesses in the market
- Know your product and services, as well as how they contribute to consumers
- Consider the overall market you are accommodating
- Analyze any data and information you have, especially performance details
- Use everything you have collected thus far to discern your true or ideal target audience

You could skip right to defining your target audience, but there's a chance you will make a mistake and focus on the wrong customers. That is why it is always a good idea to discover your market first, then move on to your target audience.

As an incredibly basic example, let's say you arre looking to target one group only. Right away - without considering your market - you could narrow things down using specifics you already know, such as males who enjoy football. Naturally, you get right to creating and managing a variety of marketing campaigns and promotions tailored to this audience.

Successful or not, this is a problematic approach. Why? Because really, you should be focused on a much broader group, like males who enjoy sports as opposed to a single activity. Unless you already have collected the necessary data, you do not know whether you are missing out on other audiences or customers just because you narrowed down your focus too quickly.

Males who enjoy basketball, soccer or even golf may also be interested in your product or service, but you ignored them by closing in on only the football group. Specifics are necessary as a last step, yes, but you want to be as accurate as possible when choosing your focus, which includes looking at a broader audience to start.

4. Build Your Target Audience

Who are your "buyer personas," or ideal customers? You need to get right to the nitty-gritty of your typical or perfect person. The more granular you can get with the information, the better. Look at traits such as:

- **Demographics:** This information can include anything from age to gender, geography to marital status.
- **Psychographics:** This information goes beyond the demographics and identifies more about a customer's psychology, interests, values, attitudes, behaviors, and much more.
- **Technographic:** This information relates to the devices. Software and other "technical" attributes of your audience.

All types of information are essential in developing your customer profiles. The demographic information will help in identifying the kind of person who will potentially buy your products and services. The psychographic information takes it a bit further and helps you to understand the reasoning behind why the customer may make the purchase. Lastly, the technographic piece helps you learn where to reach your different audiences and on what device.

Speaking of where your audience spends their time online, it is essential to find out where they hang out. What websites do they visit? Which social networks are they spending most of their time on? Do they prefer email over other forms of communication?

This helps you create the right message, and place that message in the right setting. Chances are, if your audience is not checking their email a lot, they won't see your email campaign. The information you put together for your customer profile, combined with knowing where your audience hangs out online, will improve the delivery effectiveness of your message.

Consider giving your buyer personas actual names. This will help you further distinguish them and inform your marketing plan as you create it. If you think of these personas as real people rather than a collection of traits, you will have an easier time understanding whether or not people like your buyer persona are a part of your target audience and exactly how you will target your marketing to them.

Narrow Down Your Niche

It can feel a bit counter-intuitive, but, by breaking your market down into manageable groups rather than trying to be everything to everyone, you will find greater success in reaching your audience. So how do you prevent your business from becoming the generic and mediocre all-in-one solution for everyone? Here are three ways to narrow your target market while owning your own slice of the market:

1. Commit to Your Ideal Buyer

When it comes to marketing and dominating your niche, there is no time to play games. Pick an audience and put a ring on it to get the maximum ROI out of your marketing time and money.

Even if your product or service can be tailored to fit many segments, it pays to put your stake in the ground and commit to one ideal buyer.

For instance, say you own a marketing agency. Your audience could be quite large and broad, and you could potentially serve anyone in any industry – from driving applicants to a university to helping wealth management firms find new clients. If you tried to market to every industry, your message would be quite generic: "Results-driven marketing for any entity."

Instead, your agency decides to get specific. You decide to commit your focus to higher education, narrowing your target marketing and focusing on one ideal buyer - Brenda, the CMO of a university. You get even more specific and focus on what your agency does best

– digital marketing. Now your message becomes: "Driving enrollment and increasing student ROI by helping universities get found online." It hits home for your target audience – Brenda the CMO – positioning your agency as the go-to when it comes to optimizing .edu websites for search.

Save money and time by narrowing down the focus of your target audience enough to make your message resonate with a smaller group. Although your market is smaller, you have a better chance of attracting the right buyer.

2. Refine Your Business Plan

Now that you have chosen your path, it is time to follow it to the pot of gold at the end of the rainbow. You have committed to your ideal buyer, now you need to reinforce that commitment to your business and the market place. Put your ideal buyer at the center of everything you do:

- Refine your marketing message to speak to your ideal buyer. Think about how your content strategy can tap into the pain-points of your ideal buyer and help them to solve a problem.
- Address the needs of your audience in your product/service. Build for your ideal buyer - and no one else - to create raving fans and loyal customers of your business.
- Create a customer experience that best fits your ideal buyer. For instance, if your ideal buyer is in the older demographic, they may prefer phone support to live chat or social media.

Back to our marketing agency example, once you have committed to serving Brenda the CMO, you leverage her pain-point. Brenda the CMO has a tough time managing her university's social media presence because so many participants (students, faculty, departments) are involved. So you create a free social media brand guide for higher education. The guide helps generate leads right in your target market.

On the product and service side, you decide to create a custom social listening tool that your clients can leverage to stay connected to everything faculty, staff, students and alumni are saying about their university brand. And, when it comes to client service, you know that your ideal buyer has to consistently prove ROI of marketing programs to university stakeholders. So as part of your ongoing support, you email your clients a report on their top benchmarks every week.

Putting Brenda the CMO at the center of everything you do narrows your target market, but also allows your agency to be infinitely more successful at driving leads, winning new clients and making sure they stick with your agency for a long time.

Once you have committed to your ideal buyer, follow through by integrating them into your business from product development to marketing to customer success. You will be rewarded with better leads, more customers, and increased customer lifetime value.

3. Encourage Your Evangelizers

Now that you have committed to your ideal buyer and have aligned your business to them, you are going to find yourself with some raving fans. Leverage your most enthusiastic customers to attract even more customers who are just like them.

• Run a referral campaign to ask your supporters to send new business your way. Reward them with incentives like discounts, perks and even cash money.

- Ask for reviews. If your business is on Yelp, if you have a Google listing, or if your industry has specific review sites, it can really pay off to have your customer's voices heard there, sharing their positive experience.
- Give thanks where thanks is due. When you go above and beyond for your biggest fans, they are sure go the extra mile for you – whether it's providing a testimonial, participating in a case study or being a reference.

Market segmentation can feel like a big undertaking, and can seem like a big risk since you limit your audience. However, narrowing your target market can actually give you a better chance to reach more people with a targeted message. Put your stake in the ground and commit to an ideal buyer, align your business to their needs, and mobilize your evangelizers to penetrate and conquer your niche.

Capturing Leads

Before we can talk about lead generation on social media, let's define exactly what we mean when we talk about leads. Leads are, quite simply, potential customers who have expressed some interest in your product or company and have provided contact information you can use to follow up with more information. You can then pass these leads directly to your sales department or engage with them using a tailored content marketing program.

Why is it important to think about how to generate leads on social media? Consider that 90 percent of top decision-makers say they never respond to cold calls. On the other hand, 76 percent of buyers are ready to have a conversation on social media.

If you are not providing your sales team with a steady stream of potential new customers, you are doing your business a disservice. And you are doing yourself a disservice, too, because lead generation metrics are a key way to prove the value of your social marketing efforts to your boss.

Perhaps the greatest benefit of lead generation using social media specifically is the ability to focus on highly qualified leads through advanced targeting. After all, eMarketer analysis shows that improving the quality of leads is the most significant goal for business-to-business (B2B) marketers, while simply increasing the quantity of leads comes in third.

So how do you go about using social media for lead generation? Let's look at some of the best ways to start filling the sales funnel for your team.

1. Share links to gated content

Gated content is exactly what it sounds like - content hidden behind a virtual gate. If the content is valuable enough, interested readers will be willing to provide some basic contact information in exchange for access.

When using social media for lead generation, you can promote gated content by sharing a link to a landing page where potential readers provide their information before gaining access to the content. Some people who click through to the landing page will click away without accessing your content - maybe they were mildly interested in the information but not so interested that they feel it's worth sharing their contact details. But those who are truly interested and understand that they will gain significant value are willing to overcome this minor hurdle, qualifying themselves as more than casual readers in the process.

Assuming your content is relevant to your product or industry (and it certainly should be), those interested readers who complete the landing page form become great leads. Promoting gated content directly to your followers is one of the easiest ways to gather detailed information about prospects using social media lead generation tools, so it also plays a secondary role in many of the other lead generation tactics discussed below.

Keep in mind that gated content can take several forms, and you should experiment to determine what works best with your particular audience. For B2B marketers, eMarketer analysis shows that white papers, webinars, and case studies are generally most effective.

2. Run contests

Here's the thing about contests: The prize up for grabs has to fulfill two important criteria. First, it has to be valuable enough that people will actually be interested in entering the contest. But second, it has to be valuable specifically to the people who have the highest potential to become your customers, and not much value to anyone else.

If the prize is not valuable enough, no one will enter your contest. But if it is so generically valuable that everyone who sees the contest will want to enter, you will gather loads of contact information but no qualified leads.

After all, anyone might be interested in entering a contest to win a free iPhone or trip to Hawaii, but their contact information is about as valuable as what you would find in a phone book. They have expressed no interest in you, your company, your product, or even your content - just lots of interest in big fancy free things that anyone would enjoy.

So, what should you offer as your contest prize? An extended trial of your product could be a good option, or an upgrade to a higher tier of your service. After all, those prizes only have value to people who are genuinely interested in using your product. If you sell physical products, you could give away some of the products themselves.

3. Use social media advertising

While organic social media posts can be targeted to some extent, social media advertising takes targeting and therefore the ability to collect leads from laser-focused groups of potential customers - to a whole new level. Using highly specific target audiences to promote gated content is a great way to keep advertising costs low while ensuring the leads you collect meet certain desirable criteria.

But beyond simple targeting, social media advertising has evolved to include specific social media lead generation tools: ad formats specifically designed to help marketers collect leads directly within social networks.

4. Use Facebook custom tabs

Your Facebook Business Page is a great venue for lead generation on social media. After all, data from the University of Massachusetts Dartmouth Center for Marketing Research shows that among U.S. millennials who follow brands on Facebook, 66 percent do so to get coupons or discounts, and 37 percent do so to participate in contests. That's great news for marketers, since coupons, discounts, and contests are all great social media lead generation tools.

Tabs are basically menu items that appear in the left column of your Facebook Page. Most Facebook Business Pages already use at least some of the standard Facebook Page tabs, such as About, Events, and Photos. But fewer use custom Facebook Page tabs, which can be a great way to highlight contests and offers used for lead generation on social media.

If you work with a developer, you can create custom tabs from scratch, but there are also plenty of Facebook Page apps that will help you create custom tabs, including lead generation forms, without knowing any code or investing in social media lead generation software.

5. Use targeted social media listening

Social media listening is all about keeping a virtual ear to the ground to understand what is happening in your industry, and who is talking about you and your competitors online. It is an important source of actionable insights, including potential leads who are looking to engage with businesses just like yours.

By using search streams to monitor important keywords and handles in your industry, you can uncover conversations people are having about relevant products and services, or even specific features. You can then reach out to the people behind these conversations to make a connection, share information that's helpful (maybe even gated content), and establish a relationship that will position your brand as the go-to resource when they are ready to buy.

Creating An Advertising Campaign

From talking to nonprofit and small business owners, I've learned that many think the word "campaign" is scary. To them, it sounds incredibly complicated and time-consuming - but I am here to tell you that it is not difficult to create a successful marketing campaign.

A well-planned campaign can spark new interest in your business and increase your sales, donations, and impact. In this chapter, I will give you a quick overview of what a marketing campaign is and how you can create a successful marketing campaign for your business.

I like to define a marketing campaign as a promotion created to reach a specific goal with a beginning and an end date. Your campaign can contain as few or as many pieces as you find necessary for your bottom line.

The most important part of creating a campaign is defining a clear and concise goal. Your goal can be as simple as increasing your revenue for the month of October, but it must be specific. The more specific you are when setting your goal, the greater chance you will have of actually achieving it. The specificity will help focus your tactics and save you time.

What do I need to create a campaign?

- **A way to get the word out.** Think about the most effective tools you have to spread the word about your campaign. Word of mouth, in-store signage, email marketing, and social media are great starting points — choose the tools that work best for your business.

- **A clear call-to-action.** You want to make sure your campaign has a clear call-to-action. A call-to-action encourages people to take a next step with you. You call-to-action can be anything from "download this guide now" to "make your reservation today." No matter what it is, make it as clear and easy to act on as possible.
- **A plan of attack.** Your campaign should have a start and an end date. Use a calendar to plan and plot out the important dates and actions. Here is how you might use a calendar to plan a three-part email series to promote a Valentine's Day sale. You can also use Constant Contact's new marketing calendar feature to plan your marketing, view past mailings, and check out relevant holidays.
- **Keep your ads relevant.** One way to improve relevance is to use your customers' most popular search query keywords in your ad titles and text.
- **Create multiple ads in an ad group.** Each ad group can contain as many as 100 ads (including both active and paused ads), which Bing Ads displays in an even rotation. To learn which words and phrases are most compelling to your target audience, try experimenting with a variety of ad titles and text. After you have identified your most effective ad or two in terms of CTR (click-through rate) and conversions, you can help maximize your campaign ROI by deleting the other ads from the ad group.
- **Use your customers' language.** Research the age group and gender of your typical audience, and then use that insight to write your ads. Use words and a writing tone that are likely to attract your typical customer.

- **Address your customers directly.** Use the words "you" or "your" in your ads so that you are speaking directly to them. You know what we are talking about.
- **Pre-qualify your visitors.** Use words in your ads that help attract true potential customers. For example, if you offer only high-end products, stay away from words like discount, bargain, and cheap. Be clear in your ad who your products are for. This can save you money by eliminating clicks that are not likely to convert to sales.
- **Be specific.** The clearer and more specific your offering, the better. For example, rather than "big discounts," specify an exact percentage, such as "50% off."
- **List the price of your product or service.** If your product or service is competitively priced, consider featuring the price in your ad. To help ensure that your ad gets approved, make sure that the ad links to a landing page that includes both the product (or service) and the price.

People tend to struggle most when it comes to deciding what to offer or promote in a campaign. Here are a few examples of what you can promote:

- Discounts
- Downloads
- An upcoming event
- A new service
- A free consultation
- Hints and tips
- Volunteer opportunities

Not only do you want your goals and objectives to be specific, but you want your promotion to be specific too. Telling people you have a sale going on is too vague. Telling people about a specific discount for a specific amount and product will pique their interest.

Your return on investment is very important when it comes to almost anything you do for your business. If you are unsure about the success of your campaign, you will not know if it was worth your time and effort.

Luckily, digital tools, like email marketing, make it easy to see if your campaign was a good use of your time. After sending an email, you can track your results to see how many people are opening your message and acting on your offer.

The way you measure your success will vary from offer to offer, but you always want to measure your end goal. For example, if your goal was to increase your network size, you want to take a look at how many new email subscribers you received from your campaign. If your goal was to drive attendance to your event, you should measure a number of attendees you received due to your campaign.

I know, it is a lot of information, but creating a campaign does not need to be complicated. If you are not sure where to start, think about what would be valuable to your audience and build a campaign around that.

Personalize Your Message

You may be thinking, "I'm all on board for personalizing our marketing strategy as a whole, but social media? Come on. When we're posting as a brand, how are we supposed to make each post seem personalized?"

That is an understandable objection. It feels overwhelming to think about personalizing something as real-time as social media. However, once you remember the extraordinary wealth of demographic data Facebook has on its users, the idea of personalizing your social media posts feels a lot more doable.

Facebook's data tells you all sorts of extremely detailed info about your audience, like whether people frequent organic grocery stores vs. fast food joints, or prefer crime dramas vs. reality competition TV. Then, if you pair that information with the fact that they are a dog or cat owner, a college graduate, and so on, you can easily create posts that target those specific user segments.

For example, your brand could create a post showing a dog on the couch, suggesting that users pair their next binge-watching session with your brand's organic meal kit. When a person sees something like that, it feels tailored just for them, even though it actually meets only a segment of consumers. Nearly 80% of consumers say that personalized content increases their purchase intent.

Personalizing social media isn not just expected by customers. It is also good for your bottom line:

- Once they implement personalization, over half of brands report a lift of 10% or greater across their marketing goals, with improved conversion rates and customer engagement.
- Overall consumer spending increases by 500% when personalization is launched in more channels.
- Nearly 80% of consumers say that personalized content increases their purchase intent.

Beyond revenue, a personalized marketing strategy also improves other social media metrics:

- It is engaging. The algorithmic feeds of Facebook, Instagram, and most social networks reward posts and accounts based on prior engagement by increasing their visibility in the main feed. Since personalized content is more likely to engage users, the more likely you are to organically show up in their feed.
- It builds customer loyalty. Personalized content makes a customer feel like your brand gets them and cares about them. As a result, they will feel that way towards you in return.
- It is highly shareable. Just as people like to hear about themselves, they also like to talk about themselves. No judgment here - it's just human nature. Not only will consumers be more likely to consume personalized content from your brand, they are also more likely to share it with others, building your brand awareness and attracting future customers to your social media profile.

Here are some ways you can start personalizing your strategy and messaging.

Google Adwords

Google Adwords are an amazing technique and are something worth adding to your digital marketing strategy if you have the expertise and budget. Google Adwords is for businesses wanting to display ads on Google and are largely focused on keywords. For example, if your business is focused on selling succulents, you can create an ad that pops up on Google every time consumers search for the word "succulent" or uses a phrase that contains the word "succulents."How much you pay for these ads is dependent on how competitive the keyword is, and how many other brands are using Google Adwords in your industry or niche.

In saying that, Google Adwords campaigns should only be approached if you have budget and a team that is experienced in SEM (search engine marketing) best practices and paid media to ensure you get the best results. For brands that use this strategy effectively, it can drive hundreds, thousands and sometimes even millions of dollars in revenue and ROI.

Facebook Ads with a targeted audience

Have you ever been scrolling through your newsfeed on Facebook and noticed an ad for something you have had your eye on for a while and thinking about purchasing? Whether it is a new pair of shoes, tech equipment or kitchen appliance, it's not a coincidence, that ad is targeted to you! That is Facebook ads in play and they are a great way to ensure your ads are seen by the right people.

You can also use Facebook to post specific posts to a targeted audience of Facebook users in a particular demographic, whether it's females under 25 who like fashion, or males in the USA who like sports. It is a great way to reach new audiences and it can be quite cost effective for brands who are just starting out with a paid model on Facebook.

Email segments

If you want to reach your customers on a large scale but personalize the messaging sent to them, use email marketing to target and personalize your digital marketing strategy on a whole new level. Email segments and drip-fed email marketing campaigns are based on user behaviour and triggered by pre-determined events, meaning an email is sent based on an action a user performs on your site. For example, if a new customer purchases a dress from your fashion eCommerce store, you might add them to a segment of your database of "summer clothes users" or "users who purchased dresses," so you can personalize future messaging and marketing to them based on what you know about them - they like dresses and have made a purchase from you recently.

Now that you have your segment set up and new users are being dropped into it based on their actions, you could then schedule an email newsletter for this particular segment of the list about the "Top 10 Dress Styles For Summer," because you know it is something they will likely be engaged with, so it has more chances of converting. You can do lots of personalization with email marketing, so think of ways you can segment your list and database to make the email content they receive more personalized and targeted.

Likewise, drip fed email marketing campaigns are a great way to personalize your email marketing based on segments and user behavior to give people the right content at the right time, or keep them engaged over long periods of time.

Birthday incentives and rewards

A birthday incentives or rewards program is an excellent way to make your consumer feel valued and recognized, and it is very easy to personalize the messaging with the information you have on hand. By sending them an email that is directed specifically to them with a discount code on their birthday or after they have purchased X amount of products, can turn a customer into a loyal fan. When a customer feels like a valued member of a brands community, they are much more likely to become repeat customers.

By using these steps to personalize some aspects of your digital marketing strategy, you will be able to understand your consumers on a more personal level, which ultimately allows you to personalize the marketing that is distributed to them. Consumers feel valued and your marketing is targeted – it is a win-win for everyone!

Create A Referral-Based Campaign

Referral marketing does not just happen on its own. Just like other marketing promotions, your referral program needs to be promoted and fed into your various marketing channels. Yes, referrals happen on their own through word of mouth, but how does word of mouth happen today? Social Media! In today's world of mobile apps and word of mouth marketing, the easiest way for a consumer to communicate with their friends is through social media.

As you can imagine, running a referral campaign that is social media friendly means you will have a higher chance of success. This is especially true if the business already has customers talking about them in these channels, it also makes it incredibly easy to run a social referral program.

In this chapter, we will look at effective referral marketing via social media, with some tips on how you can optimize your campaigns. A successful referral program is based on how well you promote it, and by now you realize how important social media is. But to reiterate, your customers are likely already flocking to these channels - meaning program promotion is easy.

1. Make sure you use your bio

You can let a customer know a lot about you just from using your social profiles, and a key element of focus is your bio.

Facebook provides ample room to write what you want, but Twitter likes you to keep it short and sweet. Fortunately, all you need is a link and three little words... "refer a friend". By providing easy access to the link, you're also making it easy for people to come back to it at a later time to refer.

2. Communication is key

If you are regularly checking your social media profiles, then you are probably already responding to customer feedback. Use these moments as reasons to ask for referrals. If someone mentions how much they like your service, or if they are always contributing to your page, theyare probably open to referring people to you. Communication is not just about responding though, it is about keeping your name in the conversation. Ensure you are 'share-worthy' and that your program is ready to be shared.

3. Share information about your program regularly

If you are not talking about it, how are people going to know? A good reason to regularly post about your program is that people who meant to sign up, but did not, will have the chance to di so, right at that moment, and will be able to easily find a link to your program at another time. We are not saying you need to post weekly about your program, but bringing it up every few weeks can definitely keep it fresh in people's mind.

4. Discuss exclusivity

Okay, maybe your program is not as exclusive as you lead on, but if you make it feel like a club, then people will get excited. You can boost interest by mentioning your referral program is 'by invitation only'.

Example: You post on Facebook that you are starting a referral program. You do not provide the link, instead, you talk it up and wait for people to bite. Someone comments or likes your post, and then you reach out to them personally and give them the link. You can spin this a few different ways - so long as you are pushing that not everyone gets the benefits of a program member, you should be golden.

Before you go implementing these best practices, it is important to remember that building a solid networking foundation comes first. A referral program will only work if customers believe in your business, and/or like your product to begin with.

Also, though social media is one of the easiest ways to get your program out there, it should not be the only channel you use. Customers may respond better by sharing via private email for example; this is particularly pertinent if your business is something most people consider a 'secret'. For example, people may not want everyone on their friends list to know that they have had a procedure done or bought a particular item.

With that being said, if you have customers who are online, and follow your brand, or if you have an influx of people who talk about you on their social sites, it is a pretty good indicator that social media will be a great channel for your referral program.

K. Connors

Converting Prospects Into Sales

So a lead has shown interest in your product or service, they have signed up to receive your emails and have been engaging with your communications, but how do you convert them? Here are 5 simple and effective techniques to convert warm leads into sales:

1. Offer a Product Demo or Even Better, a Free Trial

Offering a demo of your product can be an effective way to convert warm leads into sales. Showing is far more effective than telling. Prospects know that salespeople will say anything to get them to buy your product but allowing them to see for themselves what it can do is bound to spark their interest further and persuade them to buy.

Even better than a demo is a free trial. Allowing your prospects to try your product for themselves will prove to them that your product is worth investing in. If your product is a piece of software or a program, a free trial is a must for prospects. Think about it, you would not buy a brand new car without test driving it first! A lot of software companies offer 'one size fits all' demos or limited trials where the prospect only gets access to part of the system. However, we believe it is important to offer unlimited access because we like our customers to see for themselves exactly what they will be getting. With full access to your system, your prospects can experience exactly what it is like to own your product and how it can help them. Then, they are more likely to be converted.

Now, a free trial or product demo may not be possible in your industry or for your particular product but maybe you could offer a free sample, a taster session or another alternative that will entice and persuade your prospect.

2. Offer an Incentive

There is not a single person in the world that does not like a freebie. So what can you offer your prospects to entice them to buy your product? Here are a few ideas:

- A small discount
- A free E-book
- A free how-to guide
- A limited time buy-one-get-one-free offer
- A free gift
- A $10 voucher

The incentive does not have to be costly but if your prospect knows it is a limited offer, it will certainly help to speed up their decision and convert them to become a customer.

3. Show Them Your Happy Customers

According to Econsultancy, "61% of customers read online reviews before making a purchase decision, and they are now essential for e-commerce sites."

Showing off your happy customers is a great technique to use to convert warm leads into sales. By reading/hearing/seeing what a great experience your existing customers have had with your product and service, your prospect will be more likely to buy from you.

A written testimonial on your website is great but even better is a video testimonial. Video is far more convincing and believable because your prospect can put a face to a name and really see how your product has benefitted your customer and could benefit them too. (Read more about how to use testimonials in your marketing here.)

4. Concentrate On Your Email Marketing

If you know a lead is warm and just needs a small amount of extra nurturing to push them over the line, think about what they are receiving from you. Are they being sent content that is relevant for their position in your sales pipeline? What more can you do to convince them? Now could be the time to send them a personal email that really stands out because, remember, they could be shopping around for other alternatives too, and you don't want them to be snapped up by your competitor! You might include the phrase; "For more email marketing tips, click here."

5. Pick Up The Phone And Talk To Them

By picking up the phone and talking to a warm lead, you will be able to answer any questions they have and further convince them to buy. According to a study by Harvard Business Review,

> *"Companies that try to contact potential customers within an hour of receiving a query are nearly seven times as likely to qualify the lead as those that tried to contact the customer even an hour later - and more than 60 times as likely as companies that wait 24 hours or longer."*

It is important not to harass a prospect by calling them too much, but if they have a query or a question, there is no better way to respond to them than to talk to them. Remember, people buy from people and a telephone conversation offers your prospect a chance to communicate with a real person and this will certainly warm them up and convert them into a sale.

So there is our top 5 ways to convert warm leads into sales. Different techniques will work for different industries and products so it is important to try new things and find out what works best for you.

Write Social Media Copy That Sells

Do you want to create more effective social media ads? Wondering how to write ad copy that produces conversions? In this chapter, you will discover six tips for writing social media ad copy that converts.

1. Extend Your Brand Voice to Your Ad Copy

Every business needs to have its own voice, one that mimics that of its followers. When users scroll the feed, they should be able to recognize your brand voice immediately.

If your brand is more of a cargo short and t-shirt vibe, avoid using words that reflect a suit and tie mentality. The wording in your ad copy needs to mimic your other posts and include the language your demographic uses. Incorporate local lingo, slang, and grammar to match. Yes, how you spell the words in your ad makes a huge difference here.

The same goes if you are a B2B that uses more professional and business-like language when you speak and write. Mimic that style in your ad copy.

2. Clearly Communicate the Who, What, When, Where, and Why

Your social media ads not only need to include a call to action but also answer the who, what, when, where, and why. Communicating these details helps ensure users have all of the information they need to know so when they do engage with the ad, they become a warm engagement and not just a casual liker who double-taps on everything they scroll through.

47

Go back to the social media ads you are currently running. Does the ad copy answer the who, what, when, where, and why for the user? It should, and if it doesn't, pause, edit, and republish those ads.

3. Test Ad Copy Length for Performance

On some social media platforms, you have the option to use longer ad copy, but that does not necessarily mean you should use all of that real estate. If you can communicate your call to action or primary point in three to five words, do so.

Some social media experts argue that shorter copy is more effective, while others say longer copy converts better; split testing will help you discover which copy length your audience prefers. What is most important is getting to the point and ensuring users understand the message you are conveying.

4. Combine Your Copy With Complementary Visuals and Targeting

One of the reasons users flock to social media platforms is to take a break and be entertained by what they read and see. They are bored at the DMV, they are waiting for their food to arrive at the table, or their attention span of 3 seconds has expired, and it is time to look down at their phone again.

Whatever the reason, it's important that both your text and content space are harmonious. Using creativity to enhance your text is like adding extra credit points on a quiz. Your text gets the call to action (the primary point) made, but the visual further communicates that point.

Make sure all of the components of your ad (the description, headline, URL) all work together and deliver a story to users. This will make users more likely to want to learn more and not just "like" the ad.

5. Align Your Ad Copy With Specific Sales Funnel Targeting

Ad copy is essentially sales copy. But with social media ads, it cannot look or feel like sales copy at all. There is no intent on social media platforms so you cannot come in with a hard sell like you can on AdWords. That is a big reason why the conversion cycle for social media ads can take a bit longer than other marketing efforts and have more hurdles to jump through.

Summarily, a good social media ad isn not just a high-contrast image or a 45-second video. The ad copy itself can make or break engagement rates. It is time to get past the idea that we are all too busy to read.

Your ad copy needs to inform and entertain social media users to grab their attention in the news feed. If you are going to interrupt them and stop them in their scrolling tracks, give them something worth their while to look at.

Increase Customer Lifetime Value

The Customer Lifetime Value, abbreviated as CLV or LTV (for "lifetime value") is one of the most important pieces of data for your digital business. Most people who work in the e-commerce sector are familiar with notions like the cost of acquisition or the conversion rate because we are harassed by stories and theories about a recurring problem.

The goal of the CLV is to take into account your customers' loyalty and retention to calculate the turnover (or profit) that a customer will generate during his or her "life" on your site. The customer lifetime value is essential since it allows us to predict our turnover over the long term and to adjust our marketing or acquisition budget in consequence.

For this, we can suggest five concrete methods to apply as soon as possible:

Boost Your Purchase Experience

It is often said that the first and the last impressions are the ones that matter most. This is especially true in e-commerce. To increase your chances of leaving a good impression on your visitors (so they become loyal customers), it is vital that you offer the most enjoyable and smoothest shopping experience possible:

- Set up a discussion system to answer your customers' questions
- Offer free assistance and documentation (articles, guides, etc.) to help your visitors make their choice.

- Explain clearly what added value you bring to your customers; what do you do better than the competition?
- Treat your customers with love: coupons, loyalty program, etc.

Create A Stunning Newsletter

Many shopping sites' problem is that once the purchase has been made, they lose contact with their customers and rely on luck to have them buy again. This is exactly what not to do.

A newsletter (certainly not a new solution, but it is still effective) lets you keep in touch and serves as a way to convince your old customers to come back. We have already talked about retargeting (email advertising and reactivation programs) in a previous section.

Do you have a new collection coming out that you think your customers will love? Talk about it! Do you have special offers for Christmas or Black Friday? Talk about it! Did you create a super buying guide for single men? Talk about it!

- Send emails on a regular basis
- Create content with real added value for clients
- Test your email "Titles", "Subject", and "Body" (email A/B testing)

Use Upselling And Cross-Selling

To build customer loyalty and increase your average shopping cart, there's nothing like offering additional services and products. Amazon does this brilliantly, and its premium program gives access to a premium delivery service, exclusive discounts, and a video catalog with a subscription.

Involve Your Customers In All Aspects

To increase the customer's lifespan in your business, there is no secret: you must stay in touch and even seek interaction wherever possible. The key idea is to create as many interaction points in line with your business:

- Analyze your visitors online and offline activity: what do they do? Where can you find them?
- Respond to the problems they have and create content to solve their problems: are they looking for an apartment in New York? Write up a guide to real estate in NYC and share it through all the channels where they are present.
- Create a dialogue between you and your customers and encourage them to express themselves: organize competitions, quizzes, publish customer testimonials, etc.

Become A Customer Service Rockstar

Customer and after-sales service are two very powerful levers to increasing customer lifetime value. In many cases, these are the two services that transform a recent customer into a future loyal customer:

- Am I satisfied with my purchasing experience?
- Did the product or service meet my expectations?
- I had a problem with the product/service: did the brand take care of it?

By working on these levers, you increase your chances of converting your one-time buyers into regular customers; you maximize your future profits while guaranteeing a regular working capital that is much more predictable than if you have to question your acquisition budget every month.

- Listen to your customers, even the most demanding ones
- React quickly, do not let returns or complaints linger
- Publish educational and informative content
- Learn from your customers, ask for feedback
- Reward loyalty, offer benefits to your best customers
- Be transparent about the problems you encounter

Writing SEO Content

You need to balance sharing valuable content with your audiences with converting them to becoming your customers. And to do so while continually monitoring the shifting sands of online algorithms. You need to use the magic of words, images and video to turn a technically "heavy" industry into poetry for the soul.

And perhaps most challenging of all, you need to write content that satisfies the 'twin gods' of Search Engine Optimization (SEO) and social media. Your content needs to be more than searchable; it has to be shareable too.

Now, how on earth do you write to please the robot crawlers of Google and the distracted humans of Facebook?

First, let us look at some basic copywriting strategies for search engines. The main thing here is that you are catering to your user's intent, i.e., providing information or a solution that meets a specific need. Here, I will focus purely on your page content and how you can craft it to be more SEO friendly.

1. Optimize Your Title Tags/ Headlines

Also known as your headlines, these provide an indication of your page's content, and can be found between the <title> and <title> tags on the browser.

The best practice is to use phrases with the relevant keywords here (eg 8-11 words) and to keep it to 65 characters. You should try to use a mix of uppercase and lowercase characters, avoid overly commonly used titles or duplicate content (search engines prefer unique titles), and consider user intent.

2. Headings Tags

Beyond your title, do pay attention to your sub-headings and use these tags. They are important page ranking factors.

In SEO copywriting, you should only use one heading to educate readers on the topic of the page. While keywords should be in your headings, you should try not to repeat them in the heading.

Generally, keywords in the start of a heading works better. Also, avoid spamming or using irrelevant keywords in the headings – those will have a negative SEO effect.

3. Length of Content

Beyond these, do take note of the length of your content. Detailed, in-depth, and relevant content works best here.

- Educational, valuable and evergreen content are most useful
- Aim for at least 1,000 to 1,500 words if you are writing an article
- Aim for at least 500 words for other generic pages of your website
- Long content ranks better (see chart below) and could help your content be on the top 10 results on Google.

4. Optimizing Images, Videos and Audio

These days, getting your interactive media optimized helps a lot to get your results on the SERP (Search Engine Results Page). Many users love to search via using images or videos. Hence, it is important to use captions and alternate text (Alt-Text) to label your media resources carefully. Use a single keyword phrase that is relevant to your image, and ensure that your image sizes are less than 80-90 KB for optimal page-loading time.

5. Write Engaging Content

As a ranking factor, this probably trumps all the others, and for good reasons too. Content is still king, and the best forms of content will rank on the SERP. Here are some useful rules to consider to make your content engaging and enticing for both readers and search engines:

- Avoid stuffing your content with keywords – you may get penalized by search engines for it
- Use different variations of your keywords on your page in a logical way. Keep to about two or three deviations.
- Ensure that your content is informative and engages the reader.
- Update your content at least once every six months (for your website), as Google likes fresh or updated content.
- Use interactive media like images, videos and audio files on your web pages to engage users.
- Try to reduce your bounce rates and get readers to visit other pages

K. Connors

Build Your Brand

Brands often work tirelessly to leverage social media in order to boost online visibility and revenue. They want more clicks, more likes, and they want to create a positive user experience.

But what happens when a brand is a person instead of a company? When it is just you, you need to take a different approach to growing your brand through social media. Since over 90% of customers trust information from people they know when making a purchase decision, building personal connections might be the most effective way to develop trust and authority with your audience.

Here are nine ways you can use social media to make that happen.

1. Find the Right Groups

Facebook and LinkedIn both offer great opportunities to join groups focused on specific topics or industries. If you can find groups that line up with your area of expertise, then you will be able to share that experience and build authority around your personal brand.

Industry groups are good bets, but they might already be overcrowded with your competitors. Instead, think outside the box and find other groups where you are likely to find your audience.

2. Keep the Image Consistent

Across all of your social profiles, you have to maintain a certain consistency with your brand. When people want to learn more about you, they may search for you on a number of social outlets. Presenting yourself in a consistent manner helps you control their perception of your personal brand. You can damage an otherwise impeccable reputation if one of your profiles shows up with content or images that do not represent you well.

3. Engage Regularly

Building a brand takes a lot of effort, and it should be treated like a job. Every day, you should be sharing and producing content. Adjust the frequency and types of content based on the audience presence.

A once-weekly Twitter post or monthly Instagram photo are not going to accomplish much, if anything. For this reason, it is best to focus on two or three carefully chosen social networks and try to be active on them, rather than posting sporadically to a half-dozen.

4. Diversify Your Content

I recommend crafting a communications strategy for your personal brand that includes an editorial calendar and a diverse content plan so that you will not resort to publishing the same types of articles every single day. Be sure to include images, videos, articles, and even questions. I see a lot more reciprocal engagement when I change up the type of content that I post daily.

Another benefit is that this diversity prevents you from oversharing your own content. Even if your own content is fantastic, your followers will appreciate when you source and share authoritative content from other people.

5. Give as Much as You Can

If you want to create a memorable brand, you need to give people a reason to remember you. While I have grown my personal brand considerably in recent years, I still like to reach out to contacts directly and ask them what I can do for them.

You're not trying to sell or pitch anything. You're legitimately asking if there is anything you can do to help them. Give away some of your time, your advice, and any other resources you have available to help your connections. When you first start out, make it a habit to contact at least one person every day with an offer to help.

6.   Jump into Discussions

Don't be afraid to add your voice and make yourself visible in a discussion. This is especially true if you have unique insights and value to add. You will not have much luck when it comes to building your brand if you remain a wishful lurker. Being responsive will keep you on track to grow your personal brand and your network of connections.

7.   Monitor Your Name

Businesses set up all kinds of alerts for branded terms and product/service-related search phrases. Those alerts notify them when someone creates a post that includes their name or other branded terms. Do the same for your personal brand and do not forget to include alerts for common keywords involving your area of expertise. Between your alert systems and manual searches in social media, you will not miss out on opportunities to respond or join discussions.

K. Connors

Solve A Problem

People are always going to have problems, so as a marketer or business owner, your job is to solve these problems for your ideal clients. This really is the key to business success.

Here's the thing, problem-solving is easier said than done. You cannot take this lightly and cannot just go halfway with it because people will always look for better and faster ways to get what they are looking for.

It never gets easier to hear this, but at the end of the day, people do not want or care about what you sell. All they care about are that their problems are solved, and your products or services are simply a means to an end.

Some of the most successful and satisfied entrepreneurs I know figured this out early on. They were not necessarily after all the fancy bells and whistles that could have come with their products and services at the beginning. Instead, they were obsessive in solving their customer's problems. Once they figured out how to do that, they could add the "cool" factors.

Your customers don't often know how to solve their problems, but they often know what those problems are, which is why they are searching for solutions like yours. Show them that you are the answer they are looking for and have the expertise to make their pain points go away. As a marketer or business owner, that is really all you need to do.

How to discover problems

Do you have the answers to the following questions (this is a long list, but to truly be effective, you'll want the answers to each and every one of them):

- Who are you selling to?
- What are their goals and dreams?
- How do they gather information to solve their problems?
- What are some things that are important to them?
- Do you know what the biggest unmet need is in your marketplace?
- What is the biggest pain point your customers experience?
- How hard have you worked to try to solve their problems in the past?
- Why is the problem so hard for them to solve?
- Who else is trying to solve the problem and how are they approaching it?
- What does success look like to them?
- What might hold them back from buying a product or service?
- How do they come to a purchase decision?

To truly get the answers to these questions, and understand them front to back, start your research by sitting down with current customers and simply ask them some of those questions directly.

Additionally, look at online forums and sites they visit and see what they are talking about. Also take a look at your emails, look at your online reviews, and chat with your sales team to pinpoint common complaints or issues your customers are having. You will be amazed at the amount of information that can come from those sources.

How to effortlessly include problem-solving in your marketing

Refocus your messaging

Your ideal customer should always be on the top of your mind and it is imperative that your message is directed to them and resonates with them.

They want to see a message that revolves around solving their problems. It should be clear and concise so that they have little doubts as to how you can help them.

It is not uncommon for businesses to focus on themselves, products, and services in their messaging. It is important that you scan your content and refocus your message on your customers and the problems they want to be solved.

Create trigger phrases

This is a bit time consuming, but worth it. Break down the solutions you sell and the benefits of what you do. Map these back to what I like to call "trigger phrases." These should be attention grabbing statements or questions, and should come from the point of view of your customer, not your own.

Develop an attention-grabbing headline

Take a second and write a bold statement that might be the first thing anyone who visits your website will see and test this headline with your ideal clients. Ask them to be honest and detailed in their feedback. Online reviews can also provide valuable insight for writing these headlines. They can often write your promise for you.

Be educational and informative in your content

Be helpful with the content you create, even if it does not directly discuss your products or services. Show that you are knowledgeable on the issues they are facing in a variety of formats. Content is essential to any business today so get started on writing blog posts, creating how-tos, recording videos, and so on. Through content, show them that you are experts in the field that will help to make their pain points go away. Providing actionable advice can go a long way.

Make your prospects' and clients' lives easier through content upgrades

As part of your lead generation efforts, provide valuable information through content upgrades that people can download by giving at the very least their email address. This allows you to nurture them with additional helpful information down the road, which will continue to remind them that you are there for them and have the answers they are looking for.

Be responsive to comments, emails, and social media

Remember, these channels should not be one-way streets, they should be conversation tools. By responding quickly and providing thorough answers on these platforms, you are just giving them one more reason to trust you and see you as an authority in your field that has their backs.

Dive deeper than basic keywords

Keyword research is essential for speaking to and getting your audience's attention, but to really have an impact, go further than the surface level keywords and focus on long-tail keywords to really get targeted and get to the root of their problems.

Personalize your lead generation efforts

While problem solving in itself will help drive you towards success, to really make an impact in your market, you must be unique and creative in how you solve these problems because everyone in your industry is trying to address the same problems.

Create a Sense of Urgency

Imagine this scenario. You have been shopping online for a couch for weeks and you finally find the perfect one. You immediately add the couch to your cart only to find the words "Act now! Only 2 left!" alongside your dream sofa. So what do you do next? Do you turn off your computer and walk away, or do you frantically enter in your credit card number and click "Place Order" before someone else beats you to the punch? Chances are, you snatched that couch right up without hesitation.

There's a psychological reason behind why we do what we do in situations such as this. It is a key feature of the human brain and it is called urgency. Urgency is one of the most powerful forces of the human brain because it prompts us to make decisions and to act quickly. So why does urgency matter when it comes to marketing and content curation?

The answer is simple. Marketers who create a strong sense of urgency on their website, white papers, social media posts, and landing pages prompt their customers to take action. Websites that implement smart strategies relating to the psychology of urgency tend to have conversion rates that speak for themselves. There are several simple ways that marketers can prompt and accelerate their customers decision making process through the smart use of marketing tools within their content. Keep reading to find out how.

1. Create a Sense of Scarcity with Your Content

We all want what we cannot have, right? This is due to the principle of scarcity. When a potential lead is not able to obtain what they want, when they want it, it tends to make the lead want it even more. This feeling of scarcity is something you can easily create by creating a sense of scarcity with your content. This tactic is best illustrated in terms of downloadable content. If you write a fantastic white paper and upload the entire paper to a blog post, a lead could potentially just skim right past it because the content is readily available and accessible to them at any time. In contrast, if you create a blog post that teases just how incredible your new white paper is, but don't provide the actual content, your lead will likely want that content more, creating a sense of scarcity.

2. Increase Urgency Through Difficulty

This tactic may seem a bit counterintuitive but one way to create a sense of urgency in marketing is to create some level of difficulty for your lead. While we want our websites and landing pages to function smoothly and properly, the best marketers know that people value something greater if they had to work for it. This specific principle is called "The Theory of Effort Justification" and is extremely applicable to marketing. By creating a CTA button or slight obstacle between your lead and the content they want, i.e., simply filling out a form, they will not only want your content, but they will interpret it as being more valuable. Custom forms and buttons automatically increase the sense of urgency to a customer, prompting them to overcome an "obstacle" and achieve an objective.

3. Use Time-Related Words

A simple yet highly effective way to create a sense of urgency in marketing is through the use of time related words throughout your marketing content. Words like "Today" or "Download Now!" cause people to think urgently and make one more likely to take action. This is key for when you have downloadable content you want your leads to download in exchange for their email address or other information. For example, when you create a CTA (call to action) button for your latest and greatest white paper, instead of having the text simply say words such as "Download", "Read More", or "Discover" simply add a time-related word such as "Download Now" or "Contact Us Today" to create a sense of urgency. Some other examples of time-related trigger words to weave into your content and CTA buttons include:

- Instant
- Again
- Hurry
- Quick
- Rush
- Seconds
- Minutes
- Close
- Only
- Now

Now pair those words up with words like "eventually" and "later" and see how they perform in terms of creating a sense of urgency. Our point exactly! Urgency is a real thing.

One essential characteristic of a successful marketer is an understanding of how and why customers think and act the way that they do. One key psychology principle that ties into marketing is urgency. Incorporating principles of scarcity, a ticking clock, and the use of time related words will create and fuel a sense of urgency that your marketing leads simply cannot refuse.

K. Connors

Analytics of Online Marketing

Keep in mind that having the right data at hand and knowing how to analyze it is critical for any digital marketer. Because by knowing your digital marketing analytics and using them effectively can prove to be a game changer for your business.

One of the biggest advantages of doing business in the digital era is having the ability to track and analyze your results with the help of digital analytics. It gives you the needed vision to see where you are going and if your efforts are paying off. This is a luxury that you do not enjoy with traditional marketing because there simply isn't an option.

Whether it is running email marketing campaigns or just analyzing website visits, there is a vast array of information that you can decode to understand your success rate. Without a proper website in place, you would not have access to critical analytics data. Which would in turn result in lost business that cannot be regained.

A business website has become a digital marketing tool that is hard to ignore. Because it helps not only deliver information but also engagement of a high level. And in exchange of this, what your business receives is crucial data and insights that can be used to enhance your own marketing efforts and grow your business.

If your brand wants to find success with digital marketing, it needs to properly measure the effectiveness of each campaign. Because when you are clear about the ROI derived from your marketing activities, you'll know what methods/tactics to focus on. This will continue to be a challenge to all those businesses that do not work with the right data.

Every digital marketer needs to understand to go beyond digital analytics data such as bounce rate and unique visitors. There is no doubt that your analysis will always start with the basic web analytics. However, your business needs to work with rich data in order to truly understand why your marketing campaign is or is not converting. Analyzing the surface level web analytics metrics is only the first step. The next step is go deeper so that you know what your customer's journey looks like and how you can improve your sales funnel.

Digital marketing analytics allows you to get a detailed and a comprehensive understanding of how your marketing efforts are faring. It gives you an insightful view into what you can improve to get real world results from your marketing.

Your marketing almost always starts with your website, but it does not end there. With digital marketing analytics, you go beyond your website and try to understand the true effectiveness of your overall marketing efforts. By taking advantage of digital marketing analytics, you will be able to:

- Know and learn more about how each of the marketing tactics is performing. For example, is blogging giving you the needed ROI or should you focus on email marketing? Such questions can be easily answered by focusing on digital marketing analytics.
- Determine what is the true return on investment of a certain marketing initiative and if you should continue using it.
- Understand how each of your marketing activity is helping you get closer to your business objective and at what rate.

Digital marketers work with different channels. So it's important for them to use the data they get from digital marketing analytics to diagnose any problems and fix them before they get worse. These adjustments may seem trivial at first but they will have a direct impact on the overall effectiveness of your marketing.

Key Digital Marketing Analytics Metrics To Focus On

Today's consumers are looking for personalized content and solutions. Which means you need to understand everything from their goals to preferences. Only then will you be able to give them a customized experience that makes them connect with your brand and do business.

Knowing that you are getting a ton of traffic and links from other sites is great, but the question is, why? Why are people visiting your site? Why are other sites linking to you? How deeply are your visitors engaged with your content?

The answers to these questions can be found when you take full advantage and an understanding of the following digital marketing analytics.

1. Conversion Rate

When you are running a business, you want more leads and higher sales. Which is why your site's conversion rate is a metric you cannot ignore. Although this metric is all about the outcome, it can give you immense clarity on whether your traffic is targeted enough and if your marketing is helping you get closer to your business goals. Nobody likes having zero conversions or low conversions because it means your business isn't doing well.

Your conversion rate can be measured depending on what type of action you want your visitors to take. If you want more of your visitors to fill out your contact form and get in touch with you, then you need to analyze how well your traffic is converting into leads. If your goal is get sales for your product, then that is what you should focus on. The average conversion rate of your website depends on your conversion goal.

2. Days to Transaction

While impulse buying is a real thing, it rarely happens online. In other words, when someone visits your website for the first time, they may not hit the buy button right away. The time gap between their first visit and the day of their purchase can help you understand your users much better. So how do you get access to this insight?

Apply segmentation to your main traffic channels in order to get clarity on the "days to transaction" and how it differs from one channel to another. People come to your website from various channels so it is important to know what kind of traffic each channel is sending you. The higher the quality of traffic, the less will be the days to transaction.

3. Frequency And Recency

While it is nice to know how much time elapses between a visit and a purchase, it is not enough. You also need to know how frequently your visitors come to your website and what percentage of them are loyal to you. Depending on what type of site you run and how often you update it, looking into this one piece of data can help you greatly improve your site's performance.

If people consistently return to your website each time you publish a new content, great. If they just come once and leave to never come back, then you need to identify the problem areas. Loyalty is definitely a metric that you should work on improving if needed.

You can gauge how loyal your visitors are by analyzing the frequency and recency report in Google Analytics. In order to get an accurate number, make sure to exclude new users before running this report as Google Analytics tends to include them by default.

Now, we know we just threw a lot of information at you, but we are confident you can apply it to your digital marketing efforts. If you would rather have a professional analyze your data for you, no problem. There are countless resources online who will be more than happy to offer a free consultation in exchange for your potential future business.

K. Connors

Stick To Your Niche

Business owners, vloggers, bloggers, and websites all thrive on one thing; being the masters of their niche market. For some, going mainstream and facing the giants of an industry that is already saturated can work, but unless they bring value to the consumer they are going to be overlooked. While everyone goes macro, small businesses and individual bloggers must think micro when starting out. Being unique is what gets exposure, and the creativeness and passion behind what these people are trying to accomplish will show much more than those who are subconsciously more concerned about acting like or competing with the big boys.

A niche market is often overlooked by the conglomerates, bigger websites, and blogs, which opens the doors for the individual writer or small business owner. When you find that niche and get a good foothold on it, you must stick with it and grow your following and customer base without changing your identity. Too often after a year or two of success, these small businesses and blogs begin to get overconfident, and reach for consumers or viewers who are not part of the original niche they were marketing to. This eventually leads to loyal customers leaving, and what you are left with is a blog or small business that is directional-less.

You may be the captain of your ship when it comes to your business or blog, but it is the followers and customers that steer it. Ultimately it is they who take your niche market and grow it, not the other way around. When you get that strong loyal group, listen to them and they will help you get more exposure. Remember, your decision to enter a niche market has given you the opportunity to grow your business or website into something more, and if you try growing it yourself and go in the wrong direction, you are going to have many followers and customers, but they will not be loyal, nor profitable, in the long run.

Niche marketing can be profitable. If your content or products bring value to the consumer they will return, bringing more people with them the next time they visit your store or website. You built a community that was unique and brought like-minded individuals together, and now that community is growing on its own without you forcibly marketing to multiple groups. The niche market you got into has brought in niche consumers, and that is how you become successful, by naturally building off what you started and what the consumer continued.

Printed in Great Britain
by Amazon